LOVE, DAD AND me

A Father & Daughter Keepsake Journal

sourcebooks
eXplore

TO MY DAD, TOM
MY FIRST PROTECTOR,
PROVIDER, AND ROLE MODEL.
THANK YOU FOR SHOWING ME
HOW TO STRAP ON MY SKIS.

NIKLAS'S ART, AGE 4

Published by Sourcebooks eXplore, an imprint of Sourcebooks Kids.
P.O. Box 4410, Naperville, Illinois 60567–4410
(630) 961-3900
sourcebookskids.com

Source of Production: Versa Press, East Peoria, Illinois, USA
Date of Production: March 2019
Run Number: 5014253

Printed and bound in the United States of America.
VP 10 9 8 7 6 5 4 3 2 1

A GROWN DAUGHTER'S PERSPECTIVE

IT WASN'T THE FIRST TIME someone in my family crashed on the ski hill.

"I'm okay!" I shouted as casually as I could. I was about ten years old. Snow had wedged into my goggles and down my neck. My left ski had lodged itself in the hill above me like a totem pole, and I still wasn't sure where my other one had gone. I wasn't hurt—except for my pride.

"You know what?" My dad panted as he hiked to retrieve my ski. "I think I need to take a nice and easy trail next. Want to sit with me on the chairlift, Katie?"

I wiped off my tears and smiled. No one had a place in my heart quite like my dad. When I looked at him, I saw a larger-than-life hero—the smartest, strongest, funniest, kindest man on Earth. I clung to his words. I hungered for his attention and affection.

Maybe my dad felt like an ordinary man as we skied down the rest of the mountain and boarded the chairlift. But what I remember is how he and I talked about sports, school, current events, and culture. We cracked jokes. We planned ski routes. He listened to my ideas and offered guidance when I confided my fears.

I know a father-daughter relationship can feel difficult to establish or nurture. Over the years, my dad and I rode the chairlift uncountable times, and I'm sure there were moments when I only chitchatted about minutiae, while he might have been primed for great conversation. Other times, my emotions rollercoastered faster than either of us had skills to manage. And every so often, he had to sequester me from my siblings, which, at the time, I didn't always appreciate.

Now that I'm a parent, I realize how precious those one-on-one opportunities with my dad were, and I'm certain your daughter also craves more opportunities to connect with you. As her father, you set the tone for how she believes she should be treated in future relationships. You impact her self-esteem, character, behavior, and career. When it's time for her to leap from childhood to adulthood, she'll seek you because you're her dad, the man she admires most.

I have found—as have countless other parents—that keeping a parent-child journal helps us become more conscious and confident, especially when schedules are full and life feels hectic. Writing prompts offer an accessible tool that urges us to ask questions and be more aware of what our children—and we—are experiencing. This journal offers you and your daughter an inventive, lively way to connect. It's like chatting on the chairlift and skiing down. It's understanding the mountain she's afraid to tackle, confidentially discussing it together, and then cheering as she works her way down in her own unique style.

I'll never forget this past winter when my family returned to my childhood ski hill. The scenery had changed only a little: the lodge a bit bigger, the trees taller, and the two-person chairlifts replaced by triple seats.

"I think I need to ski a nice and easy trail first," my dad said. He grinned as he looked my way. "Want to sit with me on the chairlift, Katie?"

Then he looked over at my child. "You too, right?"

The three of us climbed aboard the chairlift. We were beaming! Then just like on those long-ago ski days, we began discussing the most timely topics in our lives.

Although I never shared a journal with my dad, the times we spent together connect me forever with his love. This journal is a way for you and your daughter to draw closer as you share stories, adventures, interests, and unique perspectives—to have conversations that may never surface during hectic days. As you answer prompts that make you laugh, reflect on each other's lives, or invite conversations on deeper issues, you and your daughter will navigate to a more fulfilling, understanding relationship.

These five guideposts will help you get the most from your storycatching time together.

❶ Use this journal your way.

Start at the front and work through the pages in order, or flip through the journal and answer any prompt that intrigues you and your daughter. Answer the questions together over scoops of ice cream or pass the book back and forth, making entries in turn. Write as much or as little as you want. Add or alter anything. If a prompt doesn't resonate with you, cross it out and write in your own, or cover it with a photograph or drawing.

Your daughter's thoughts go on pages that begin "Dear Daughter" or "Daughter Writes." Corresponding "Dear Dad" and "Dad Writes" pages are your opportunity to reply or launch another conversation. Intermixed throughout are spaces to write, doodle, and adhere keepsakes together.

❷ WRite WitH autHenticity.

A story doesn't have to be perfect to be impactful, and neither do you. Write what you know, model your values, and demonstrate to your daughter that imperfection in both life and writing is okay.

My journals are speckled with blemishes: crossed-out words, bumbling sentences, and spelling errors that would make my fourth-grade teacher cringe. But I keep writing because I have found that jotting down some story—no matter how insignificant my thoughts may seem—is infinitely better than sharing nothing.

❸ Become an engageD listeneR.

Try to understand what your daughter is really communicating. Does she want you to change things for her, or does she actually need you to just lend an ear as she sorts stuff out?

Sharing this journal gives you both a peek inside one another's heads and hearts. Some entries address things you already know. Others can help you discover emotions or entire stories that you weren't aware of. Respond immediately or walk away and ruminate for a while. Appreciate that your daughter may have stories she's not comfortable communicating yet. Be patient and keep listening.

❹ Play.

This journal is a home for words, but it's also a place to play! Doodle. Trace your hands. Write, underline, and circle words with different pens. Add colorful speech bubbles and borders, or draw details using only black and white. Decorate with stickers and gathered mementos. Snap pictures together and adhere them with glue or double-sided tape. Above all, enjoy yourselves.

❺ Go Beyond these Pages.

Your father-daughter journaling experience only begins in this journal. You're warmly welcome to explore my exclusive *Love, Dad and Me* resources, including creative father-daughter Saturday-night-in ideas, journaling jokes your daughter will love, and examples from my own journals on:

katieclemons.com/a/xw6n

I'd love to hear how your journal is coming together. Drop me a note at **howdy@katieclemons.com** (I answer all my mail) or join me on social media **@katierclemons, #katieclemonsjournals,** and **#lovedadandme**.

Imagine opening this journal in ten or twenty years and reviewing it with your now-grown daughter. You'll see pages filled with stories and perspectives, youthful penmanship recording moments you haven't thought about in years, photographs, illustrations, and best of all…reminders of how much you love each other.

YOU'RE A GREAT DAD. Snap on some skis, hit the trail, and… Let's celebrate your story! ♡ Katie

Here's a photograph or drawing of

YOU  & Me

HELLO ♡ WORLD!

Our full names are

_____

_____

We sign our names like this

_____

_____

We call each other

_____

_____

We are _____ and _____ years old.

TODAY, WE LAUNCH THIS JOURNAL!

 Date _____

OUR JOURNAL
GUIDELINES

❶ Is our journal top secret or can anyone else look inside?

❷ If someone finds this journal, they should

☐ Return it

☐ Complete it

☐ Destroy it

☐ Share pages online

☐ Hide it in _____

☐ Sell it for $ _____

☐ Turn it into a _____ movie

❸ Do we have to answer prompts in numerical order?

☐ Yes   ☐ No

4 Our top focus(es) in this journal will be to

☐ Express our thoughts

☐ Use perfect grammar

☐ Capture memories

☐ Skip our responsibilities such as _____

_____ in order to write

☐ _____

☐ _____

5 How much time do we have to write before passing our journal back to one another?

6 What could we do if we need more space to write?

7 Is there a specific date when this journal must be complete?

8 How do we pass our journal back and forth?

9 How should we tell each other which page to turn to?

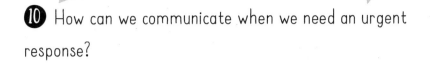

10 How can we communicate when we need an urgent response?

11 Are there other guidelines we should establish for our journal?

DEAR **DaD,**

What's something I do that makes you happy?

DEAR **Daughter,**

What's something I do that makes you happy?

"TIME FOR A HUG!"

you me

Our excited faces

DAD

DAUGHTER

Our frustrated faces

DAD

DAUGHTER

Our laugh-until-we-cry faces

DAD

DAUGHTER

WE WRITE

Daughter WRITES

Dad, the first thing you say to me in the morning is

The last thing you say to me before bed is

 # Dad WRITES

Daughter, the first thing you say to me in the morning is

The last thing you say to me before bed is

DEAR DAUGHTER,

What are three of your proudest accomplishments?

1

2

3

Is there another goal you want to achieve?

DEAR **DaD,**

What are your thoughts on what I wrote about my achievements?

Do you think I can accomplish my goal?

DaugHteR WRITES

Our family

Our community

Outside our house

Inside our house

DaD WRITES

Our family

Our community

Outside our house

Inside our house

GREAT THINGS WE'VE DONE
TOGETHER

1

2

3

4

WE WRITE

Date

EXCITING THINGS WE STILL NEED TO DO
TOGETHER

1 _____

_____

_____

_____

2 _____

_____

_____

_____

3 _____

_____

_____

_____

4 _____

_____

_____

_____

DaugHteR WRITES

Dad, you are handsome inside and out because

①

②

③

④

⑤

Here's a picture of you,

MY _____ DaD.

→→→ This is you ←←←

☐ belly laughing
☐ being brave
☐ acting silly
☐ handing me _____
☐ attempting great things

☐ loving me, your daughter
☐ looking serious
☐ spreading joy
☐ _____
☐ _____

Dad WRITES

Daughter, you are beautiful inside and out because

1

2

3

4

5

Here's a picture of you,

MY _____ DaughteR.

⟫⟫⟫———▷ This is you ◁——⟪⟪⟪

☐ belly laughing

☐ being brave

☐ acting silly

☐ doing chores without reminders

☐ attempting great things

☐ looking serious

☐ spreading joy

☐ loving me, your dad

☐ _____

Daughter WRITES

I look forward to the holiday season because

_____

_____

_____

_____

I remember one time when

_____

_____

_____

One of my favorite traditions is

_____

_____

_____

_____

Our house looks like

Our house smells like

People who make the season magical

I love these food traditions

DaD WRITES

When I was growing up, I remember looking
forward to the holiday season because

_____

_____

_____

_____

One of my favorite traditions was

_____

_____

_____

I remember one time when

_____

_____

_____

_____

Our house looked like

Our house smelled like

People who made the season magical

I still cherish the memory of these foods

DEAR DAUGHTER,

Tell me about a time you did something kind for someone else when didn't have to.

AWESOME SPOT TO DRAW.

HIGH FIVE!

Why did you do it?

How did it make you feel?

DEAR DaD,

What are your thoughts on kindness?

GREAT SPOT
TO DOODLE.

Do you have a story of when you saw me being kind?

you ❤ me

Right now, we're listening to

DAD

DAUGHTER

We're reading

DAD

DAUGHTER

We're watching

DAD

DAUGHTER

WE WRITE

DAD WRITES

Daughter, I admire these traits about you

1

2

3

DAUGHTER WRITES

Dad, I admire these traits about you

1

2

3

DEAR Dad,

What were you like when you were my age?
What was your life like?

DEAR Daughter,

How is your life different from
and similar to when I was a kid?

DEAR DAD,

Tell me a story about when I was little.

Date

TIME TO SAY
"I LOVE YOU."

DEAR Daughter,

Do you have any questions about boys?

How do you believe girls and women deserve to be treated?

Do you ever see people doing something different?
How do you feel about that?

DEAR Dad,

What are your thoughts on what I wrote?

_____

_____

_____

_____

How do you believe girls and women deserve to be treated?

_____

_____

_____

_____

Do you ever see people doing something different? How do you feel about that?

_____

_____

_____

_____

Here's a picture of
YOU  me
relishing winter.

We give winter ☆ ☆ ☆ ☆ ☆ stars!

 FILL IN FOR
RATING.

WE WRITE

- [ ] We love this season!
- [ ] Okay, winter gets kinda long.
- [ ] LET IT SNOW!
- [ ] We should move somewhere _____ er.
- [ ] We have/haven't had enough snow days.
- [ ] Pour us another mug of _____.
- [ ] We can't feel our toes.
- [ ] Winter is warm here!
- [ ] _____

Brrrr!

Our winter theme song should be

The best things to do each winter are

1 _____

2 _____

3 _____

4 _____

5 _____

DEAR Dad,

What are three of your proudest accomplishments?

1 _____

_____

_____

2 _____

_____

_____

3 _____

_____

_____

Is there another goal you want to achieve?

_____

_____

_____

_____

DEAR **DAUGHTER,**

What are your thoughts on what I wrote about my achievements?

Do you think I can accomplish my goal?

Date

 DEAR Dad,

Tell me about a special gift I made you
when I was younger. Do you still have it?

Could you draw a picture?

DaD WRITES

DEAR Daughter,

What kinds of things do you like to make now?

Could you draw a picture?

DEAR Daughter,

What are four things you secretly wish you could do?

1

2

3

4

DEAR Dad,

What do you think about the four things I wrote?

Was there anything you wished
you could do and then you did it?

you ♥ me

What would we do if we had the whole day together with no work or chores?

DAUGHTER

DAD

WE WRITE

DAD WRITES

Daughter, I
know you love me
so much because

DAUGHTER WRITES

Dad, I know
you love me so
much because

DEAR DAUGHTER,

Tell me about a school subject that's difficult for you.

Why do you think it feels so challenging?

How can I help make it easier for you?

DRAW HOW
YOU FEEL
ABOUT IT.

DEAR **DAD**,

What do you think of what I wrote about school?

PERFECT TIME FOR A HUG.

Which subject did you struggle with
when you were my age?

How does knowing that subject help you now?

you ❤ me

Five things we can't live without

DAUGHTER

DAD

WE WRITE

DEAR **DAD,**

How did I get my name?

DEAR **Daughter,**

I have a question for you

_____

_____

_____

Daughter WRITES

Date

DaD WRITES

Daughter, I always hear you say these phrases

DaughteR WRITES

Dad, I always hear you say these phrases

DaD WRITES

Daughter, I'm really proud to be your dad because

_____

_____

_____

_____

I would describe you as a person who

_____

_____

_____

You make me feel special when

_____

_____

_____

_____

Date

DAUGHTER WRITES

Dad, I'm really proud to be your daughter because

_____

_____

_____

I would describe you as a person who

_____

_____

_____

You make me feel special when

_____

_____

_____

DEAR Dad,

What are some of your favorite parts of being a parent?

NICE SPOT
TO DOODLE.

Date

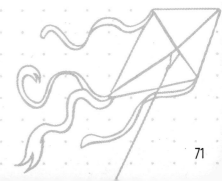

DEAR Daughter,

What do you think about what I wrote on being a parent?

Do you think you want to be a parent someday?

you ♥ me

Our favorite game is

DAD

DAUGHTER

The best book is

DAD

DAUGHTER

The _____est TV series is

DAD

DAUGHTER

DEAR Dad,

What was your first email address?

What did you use it for?

Step-by-step, how did you check your email?

1 _____

_____

2 _____

_____

3 _____

_____

DRAW YOUR PHONE HERE.

When did you get it?

What did you use it for?

Was there anywhere that your cell phone didn't work?

DEAR **Daughter,**

Record your current email or username here.

How did you get that name?

What platforms do you use it for?

How do you use those platforms and how often?

DRAW YOUR DEVICE HERE.

Do you ever feel pressured or
uncomfortable about anything online?

Is there anything I can do to help you when that happens?

DEAR Dad,

What are your thoughts on what I wrote about feeling pressure or discomfort?

Daughter WRITES

Dad, in 30 years, you'll be _____ years old. If you
remember just one thing about who I am today, I hope it's

_____

_____

_____

_____

_____

_____

Dad WRITES

Daughter, in 30 years, you'll be _____ years old. If you
remember just one thing about who I am today, I hope it's

_____

_____

_____

_____

_____

_____

Here's a picture of **you & me** having fun when we were younger.

you  me

What we look like dancing

What we look like sleeping

What we look like running late

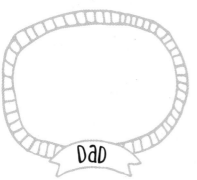

DaD WRITES
My typical weekday

6:00 _____

7:00 _____

8:00 _____

9:00 _____

10:00 _____

11:00 _____

NOON _____

1:00 _____

2:00 _____

3:00 _____

4:00 _____

5:00 _____

6:00 _____

7:00 _____

8:00 _____

9:00 _____

10:00 _____

DAUGHTER WRITES
My typical weekday

 Date

6:00 ....

7:00 ....

8:00 ....

9:00 ....

10:00 ....

11:00 ....

NOON ....

1:00 ....

2:00 ....

3:00 ....

4:00 ....

5:00 ....

6:00 ....

7:00 ....

8:00 ....

9:00 ....

10:00 ....

DEAR **DaD,**

I have a question for you

_____

_____

_____

Here's a picture of
you  me
soaking up summer.

We give summer ☆☆☆☆☆ stars!

FILL IN FOR
RATING.

WE WRITE

☐ We love this season!

☐ Summer's just not long enough.

☐ LET THE SUN SHINE.

☐ The air conditioner is running.

☐ We should vacation somewhere _____ er.

☐ Give us all the icy _____ to drink.

☐ We own _____ bottles of sunblock.

☐ _____

Our summer theme song should be

The best things to do each summer are

❶ _____

❷ _____

❸ _____

❹ _____

❺ _____

you ♥ me

We could spend the whole summer
together doing nothing but

DaUGHTeR

DaD

WE WRITE

you ♥ me

On our feet today

DAD

DAUGHTER

On our heads

DAD

DAUGHTER

In our pockets

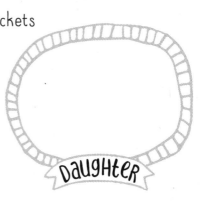

DAD

DAUGHTER

DEAR Daughter,

Do you have any questions about growing up?

Is there anything you feel nervous about?

DEAR **DaD,**

What do you think about what I just wrote?

DEAR Daughter,

Tell me about a sport that you enjoy.

What do you like about it?

How does it make you feel?

DEAR Dad,

What are your thoughts on what
I just wrote about sports?

Tell me about a sport you really enjoyed
when you were my age.

you ♥ me

We love these jokes

WE WRITE

Date

TIME FOR
A LAUGH!

95

DaD WRITES

Daughter, three words I'd use to describe you are

1 _____

2 _____

3 _____

I've always admired how you

_____

_____

_____

I'll always ask your advice on

_____

_____

_____

I hope that you never stop

_____

_____

_____

Daughter WRITES

Dad, three words I'd use to describe you are

1 ....

2 ....

3 ....

I've always admired how you

....

....

....

I'll always ask your advice on

....

....

....

I hope that you never stop

....

....

you ♥ me

The bravest person we know

DAD

DAUGHTER

The most generous person we know

DAD

DAUGHTER

The funniest person we know

DAD

DAUGHTER

DEAR **Dad,**

Do you vote? Why or why not?

What do you think makes a good candidate?

DAUGHTER WRITES
My favorite HOLIDAY is

because _____

_____

_____

_____

_____

_____

Here's us CELEBRATING!

DaD WRITES
My favorite HOLIDAY is

because _____

Here's us **CeLeBRaTiNg!**

DEAR Daughter,

Tell me about a hobby you enjoy.

How did you get interested in it?

What do you like about it?

What's challenging right now?

How would you rank this hobby?

I give this hobby ☆☆☆☆☆ stars!

FILL IN FOR RATING.

DEAR **Dad,**

Tell me about a hobby you enjoy.

How did you get interested in it?

What do you like about it?

What's challenging right now?

How would you rank this hobby?

I give this hobby  stars!

FILL IN FOR
RATING.

DaughTer WRITES

I always look forward to

DaD WRITES

I always look forward to

DEAR _____ ,

I have a question for you

_____

_____

_____

WE WRITE

DaugHteR WRITES

Here's a keepsake from my life right now

It's a

- ☐ ticket stub
- ☐ receipt
- ☐ wrapper
- ☐ thing from school
- ☐ quote or poem
- ☐ list or note from my pocket
- ☐ photo or picture
- ☐ _____

I'm adding it to our journal because

DaD WRITES

Here's a keepsake from my life right now

It's a

- ☐ ticket stub
- ☐ receipt
- ☐ wrapper
- ☐ newspaper clipping
- ☐ quote or poem
- ☐ list or note from my pocket
- ☐ photo or picture
- ☐ _____

I'm adding it to our journal because

DEAR Daughter,

Do you remember a story from when you were little?

Dad WRITES

The money we have has enabled our family to

These are times when money doesn't matter to our family

I think it's important to set aside money for

I enjoy giving time or money to

DauGHteR WRITES

The money we have has enabled our family to

_____

_____

_____

_____

These are times when money doesn't matter to our family

_____

_____

_____

I think it's important to set aside money for

_____

_____

_____

I enjoy giving time or money to

_____

_____

_____

_____

DEAR **DaD,**

What was your favorite job before I was born?

How old were you? And how much did you get paid?

How did you travel to work?

What were your responsibilities?

Why did you like the job?

Tell me about a mistake you made or
lesson you learned at this job.

DEAR Daughter,

What do you think about my favorite job?

Would you try it?

What kind of jobs do you want
to experience?

Tell me about the kind of life you dream
of having when you're grown up.

DEAR DAD,

Tell me about an older relative that
I didn't get to know well.

ADD MEMORIES
AROUND THE
PICTURE FRAME.

Daughter WRITES

Two things you did that made me laugh
or smile this past week, Dad

1 _____

_____

2 _____

_____

Two things other people did that made me
happy this past week

1 _____

_____

2 _____

_____

 Two things I did this past week that hopefully
brought other people joy

1 _____

_____

2 _____

_____

DaD WRITES

Two things you did that made me laugh
or smile this past week, Daughter

1 _____

_____

2 _____

_____

Two things other people did that made me
happy this past week

1 _____

_____

2 _____

_____

Two things I did this past week that hopefully
brought other people joy

1 _____

_____

2 _____

_____

 you ♥ me

Something we own that's blue

 DAD

 DAUGHTER

Something we've kept that's old

 DAD

 DAUGHTER

Something we just bought ourselves

 DAD

 DAUGHTER

Dad WRITES

Daughter, when you're _____ years old like I am now,

make sure you take time for yourself to

_____

_____

_____

_____

_____

Daughter WRITES

Dad, when I'm _____ years old like you are now,

make sure you take time for yourself to

_____

_____

_____

_____

_____

DEAR **DaD,**

Tell me about the first time you held me.

TIME TO SAY
"I LOVE YOU!"

you & me

WE'RE GRATEFUL FOR...

This place

DAD

DAUGHTER

This activity on the calendar

DAD

DAUGHTER

This object in our house

DAD

DAUGHTER

DAUGHTER WRITES
FUTURE PREDICTIONS

YOU AND ME IN _____ YEARS

Dad, I anticipate you won't have to spend
any more time on

_____

_____

_____

You'll have more time to

_____

_____

You'll be really good at

For your birthday, you'll want

I'll probably give you

I'll have to start reminding you to

Most likely, you'll still be reminding me to

We'll continue to tell each other

DAD WRITES
FUTURE PREDICTIONS

YOU AND ME IN _____ YEARS

Daughter, I anticipate you won't have to spend
any more time on

_____

_____

_____

You'll have more time to

_____

_____

You'll be really good at

For your birthday, you'll want

I'll probably give you

I'll have to start reminding you to

Most likely, you'll still be reminding me to

We'll continue to tell each other

Daughter WRITES

I regularly forget

I always remember

 # Dad WRITES

I regularly forget

I always remember

you ♥ me

Right now, we're thankful for

DAD

DAUGHTER

We're curious about

DAD

DAUGHTER

We're saving up for

DAD

DAUGHTER

DEAR Daughter,

On a scale of 1 to 5, how do you feel about yourself?

How happy are you with your life?

Tell me more.

DEAR DAD,

What are your thoughts on what I just wrote?

i ♥ u

PERFECT TIME
FOR A HUG.

DEAR _____,

I have a question for you

_____

_____

_____

DaD WRITES

Daughter, let me trace your hand here.

DAUGHTER WRITES

Dad, let me trace your hand here.

you ♥ me

Things we collect

DAD

DAUGHTER

Things we never keep

DAD

DAUGHTER

The most sentimental thing we own

DAD

DAUGHTER

Date

DEAR **Daughter,**

Tell me what's on your mind.

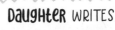

Date

you & me TOGETHER